The Science of Mindleading
Volume I

The Fundamentals

I0447762

by Felix Brocker

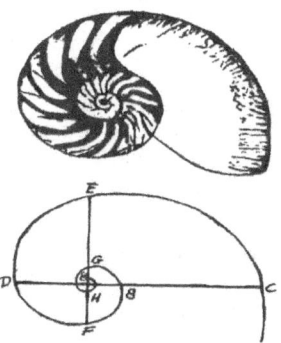

The Nautilus is growing at a constant rate, and thus forms its shell a logarithmic spiral to accommodate this growth without changing the shape. A lifeline connects its chambers, so that the previous chambers are left behind, but will never be forgotten. The Nautilus constantly creates new wider chambers in perfect proportion. Despite the profound changes around it, the Nautilus continues to thrive.

It reminds us that advancement is a part of the creation of the universe. The Nautilus is a symbol of a rigorous scientific research and the interdisciplinary nature of the sciences.

Bibliographic Information

The Science of Mindleading®
Volume 1 - The Fundamentals

by Felix Brocker

ISBN-13: 978-1479145454
ISBN-10: 1479145459

science-of-mindleading.com

facebook.com/mindleading

twitter.com/mindleading

Copyright © 2014

Felix Brocker, Nelsenstr. 17e, 41748 Viersen, Germany

All rights reserved.

Translated from the German original "Die Wissenschaft der Gedankenführung Band 1 Grundlagen" by Felix Brocker

Also available as an ebook.

This book is published with help of CreateSpace Independent Publishing Platform. It is in its entirety copyrighted. Any use outside the limits of copyright law, without the prior consent of the author, is prohibited and may be prosecuted. This applies in particular to duplications, translations, adaptations and modifications. The images that are used in this book are, with the exception of the cover image royalty free. They are taken from the free encyclopedia wikipedia and its sister site wikimedia.

TABLE OF CONTENTS

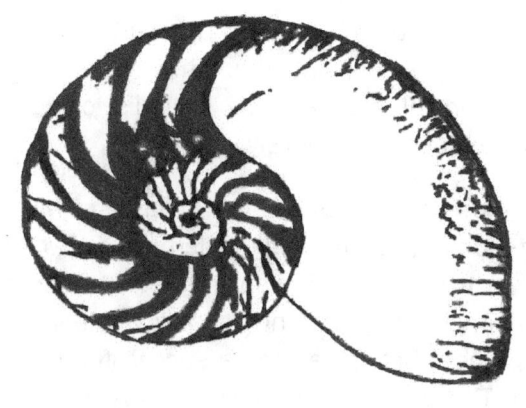

1. THE SCIENCE OF MINDLEADING

The question of whether there may be a "Science of Mindleading" can undoubtedly be answered in the affirmative. In this scientific context, the concept of mindleading means the ability of a man to guide his own thoughts in a certain way.

The outstanding importance and the urgent need for a Science of Mindleading is clear from its initial question, which is:

What drives the successful and happy people to accomplish over and over again top performance?

Accurately can also be asked, "Why is a man of success in life, while the other always fail in everything he does? Why a man is always hale and hearty, while the other is plagued by an illness after another? Why is one man filthy rich, and the other remains despite working hard all his life poor?" This list of questions could go on and on endlessly yet.

On all these critical issues, the Science of Mindleading intends to find knowledgeable answers to demonstrate to the individual, who maybe is unsuccessful and unhappy, as by learning the ability to lead his own mind properly,hot to become a successful and happy people. The essential and incredibly valuable knowledge of the Science of Mindleading is as follows:

Only the one, who is able to lead his own thoughts properly, can act in every situation in the most rational and therefore always in the most effective manner. The person, however, who is not able to lead his thoughts, but whose thoughts lead him acts uncontrolled and mostly irrational and ineffective.

This means that the idea is to keep a person in a position where he is able to reach incredible heights. However, the thoughts of a person unguided occur sometimes in the most brutal form, and set up within society an immense damage. The results of a Science of Mindleading are therefore invaluable, both to the individuals and to the community.

The Science of Mindleading intends both, to clarify the question of how man leads his thoughts on the best and most beneficial and secondly, it should explore the limits of the possibilities guided thoughts, if they exist at all.

The elaboration of the fundamentals of mindleading works with a cross section through the established and recognized sciences. This cross-section through all the sciences makes the operation and a highly interdisciplinary of a Science of Mindleading already very clear. It evaluates the findings of the recognized sciences and links them together. Hence the Science of Mindleading is not a science in the traditional sense, since it does not conduct research itself.

But it can therefore be described as science, however, because the results of a rigorous scientific research are used to be put in an entire new context. And so, despite the breakdown of the chapters of this book to each separate sciences, always a connection with at least one other scientific discipline can be produced.

We begin with a look at the history to clarify the question of whether in the past, people have dealt with the question of a possible mindleading and if so, to what conclusions they came. Then we consider the mindleading of both philosophically and religiously, in order to clarify fundamental issues in particular in relation to the power of the faith and of the mind. After clarifying the basic "faith issues", the other recognized sciences follow. Special attention is paid to the psychology, the neurology and the most important findings of brain research.

This book approaches the idea of mindleading as a science not in a strictly scientific approach. For example, you won`t find references in footnotes, but within the text.

Now that you know what the Science of Mindleading is about and what goal this science pursues, we introduce the study of its fundamentals with a very promising view on the history.

2. HISTORY

The first question that imposes itself a nearly, is whether in the past, people have dealt with the topic of "mindleading".

Thanks to the internet, we come fairly quickly to a wide variety of quotes from great and important figures in history. These quotes can be, like a puzzle consisting of many individual parts, put together into a larger whole.

So said about the writer J.W. Teal, "It is the habitual thought that frames itself into our life. It affects us even more than our intimate social relations do. Our confidential friends have not so much to do in shaping our lives as the thoughts have which we harbor."

How much we are actually influenced by our habitual thoughts, shows the following quote by Buddha.

"All that we are is the result of what we have thought. The mind is everything. What we think we become."

Not only isolated quotations can be found, but there is a whole movement that has dealt with the issue in the broadest sense of "mindleading". Of particular interest is the American "New Thought Movement".

This movement emerged in the second half of the 19th Century in the United States of America from the teachings of the healer and writer Phineas Parkhurst Quimby and the transcendental philosophy of Ralph Waldo Emerson.

Quimby took a view that was strongly influenced by Christianity. He always referred to the mind of God who demands nothing but kindness and harmony. All the evil in the lives of men are only the consequences of negative thoughts. Thus the New Thought Movement, which is in origin Christian nature, is often classified as a spiritual or religious group.

The flagship of the American New Thought Movement was the journal "The Nautilus - Magazine of New Thought", which was published from 1898 to 1953 by

Elizabeth Towne and her husband William Towne. The nautilus is a primordial sea creature that lived back in the depths of the sea, when the earth was still a single large continent. The nautilus is growing at a constant rate, and its shell forms a logarithmic spiral. So it can absorb its constant growth without changing its original shape. A lifeline connects its chambers, so that the previous chambers are left behind, but will never be forgotten. The nautilus constantly creates new wider chambers in perfect proportion. And despite the profound changes around it, the Nautilus continues to thrive. It reminds us that growth is part of the creation of the universe. The nautilus reflects symbolically the motives of the American New Thought Movement.

In almost every issue of the Nautilus-Magazine, an article of the book author Wallace Delois Wattles was published. His most famous work, "The Science of Getting Rich" was published in 1910 by Elizabeth Towne Publishing, one year before he died.

Wattles was born in 1860, just before the outbreak of the Civil War, as the son of a gardener and a home-maker. And so, even as his father, Wattles first was a farm worker. He bled himself and his family more bad than good through life. At that time, his life was marked by defeats, losses, poverty and failures. Just problems at all. And in his life for a long time, nothing has pointed out that he should ever attain great wealth.

During the Christmas season 1896 Wattles visited at the age of 36 years, a meeting at which he was con-fronted with a kind of Christian socialism. The theo-ries, raised there, must have exerted great influence on him. He busied himself henceforth on a fundamen-tal way with how he could lead himself and his family out of poverty towards prosperity. When he thought he had found the key to a successful and happy life, he started in almost every free moment to write. Wattles rapidly became one of the most important writers of the American New Thought Movement. He practiced his own theories with success, and he became a suc-cessful, prosperous and strong personality full of ener-gy.

The Science of Mindleading Special Issues contain his three most important books and are an addition to this chapter. Wattles books are purely pragmatic. This means that they show their readers how to lead his mind by recognizing certain statements as absolutely true. The reader shall make his firm conviction, but shall not even begin to question. The reader must rec-ognize the following statements, according to Wattles, to be absolutely true, in order to lead his mind on the proper way,

"There is a Cosmic Intelligence that is in all things and through all things. This is the one real substance. From it all things proceed. It is Intelligent Substance or Mind Stuff. It is God. Where there is no substance there can be no intelligence; for where there is no substance there is nothing. Where there is thought there must be a substance which thinks. Thought cannot be a function; for function is motion, and it is inconceivable that mere motion should think. Thought cannot be vibration, for vibration is motion, and that motion should be intelligent is not thinkable. Motion is nothing but the moving of substance; if there be intelligence shown it must be in the substance and not in the motion."

3. PHILOSOPHY

According to historical evidence, now the philosophy follows.

The philosophical insights logically follow as a second, because ultimately it is the philosophy that tries to explain the world and the human existence with the help of the mind. Therefore, philosophy is addressed not only in this chapter, but also in others, particularly in the fifth chapter, which will deal briefly with the mystery of human consciousness.

After having read the previous chapter "History", we are interested in, whether all around us and even we ourselves are created from the same substance that can think beyond even.

This key question, which we will discuss mainly in this philosophical chapter introduces us to the Transcendental philosophy of Ralph Waldo Emerson and the so-called monism.

3.1 The Philosophy of Ralph Waldo Emerson

The transcendental philosophy of the American philosopher and influential writer Ralph Waldo Emerson coined the new thoughts of the American New Thought Movement at that time very much.

Emerson's first book "Nature", published in 1836, contains several essays in which he believes that people should live in a simple way with themselves and with nature.

His lectures at the Harvard University in 1828 led to his suspension. But especially around his students his lectures were widely acclaimed. After Emerson's suspension they joined the club of the transcendentalists and Emerson quickly became the leader of the Transcendental Movement. Emerson's philosophy is strongly monistic.

3.2 The Philosophical Monism

In philosophy, it is often the talk about that the world consists of substances. In the philosophical discussion, essentially two different views face each other, the monism and dualism. While the monism presupposes the existence of a single substance, the dualism assumes that there must be at least two substances, the matter and the mind.

Already in ancient Greece the known natural philosophers and mathematicians believed to have found a primary substance, at Thales it was the water, at Anaximenes it was the air and at Pythagoras it were numbers. The philosopher Democritus was already of the opinion that the world consists of clusters of very small parts, the atoms.

Known representatives of monism were the European philosophers Thomas Hobbes and Spinoza. Other well-known representatives of monism are the philosophers Descartes, Leibnitz, Schopenhauer and Hegel.

In the chapter "Nature Sciences", we will refer to the search of this one substance, from which the philosophers speak, again.

4. RELIGION

The religion permeates every society. It heals the soci-ety`s wounds, but sometimes the religion drives deep wedges into it and splits a society.

The issue of religion is so delicate that at first some preliminary observations are appropriate.

This book is, despite some clear words, neither a judg-ment of the various religions, nor does it dictate his readers exactly what they must believe. This book aims to stimulate its readers merely to reflect their own thinking as well as the thinking of other people.

Therefore it is inevitable to examine religion, that shapes the thinking and the lives of very many people, critically.

In detail the critical examination of religion, we have to determine that people who are driven by a solid unshakeable belief, can sometimes move mountains sometimes.

This deep religious belief manifests itself in various forms, that are explained in greater detail.

The first form, we will take a closer look at, are the religious miracles.

4.1 Religious Miracles

Since always, diverse religious miracles have been making a name for themselves.

A religious miracle is a positive event in the field of religion, which can be explained by no one and leaves us wondering and wondering. This kind of miracles is particularly widespread in Christianity, surprisingly far. The lame can suddenly walk again and the blind can, oh divine miracle, see again.

All this may simply sound biblical and untrustworthy. But still, they really do exist, these religious "miracle cures" that leave us amazed and sometimes puzzled.

But what is it really, that surprises and puzzles us?

What lets us marvel at the religious miracle cures actually is the power of the deep-rooted faith in a man. It is not the power of a saint, nor is it the power of God that is able to heal the sick. It is the sectarian faith of man in a speedy recovery.

This unshakable belief in the occurrence of recovery is so powerful that ultimately encourages it's own disease-ridden body to heal itself successfully. It is not the placing of a sacred hand, but it is the fixed and unalterable belief in the occurrence of recovery, that leads to the result that your own body begins to heal itself.

This interesting phenomenon of a spontaneous self-healing will be discussed as the placebo effect in the sixth chapter "Medicine" in more detail, because in this case it is also the firm and unshakable belief in the incoming healing, that causes that your own body begins to finally heal itself.

About the religious miracles, we can conclusively say that these miracle cures are very welcome events, in which the power of one's faith gets very clear.

Another religious phenomenon, that we can not view as particularly welcome, is the religious self-flagellation.

4.2 Mortification and Absolute Sacrifice

Believers of various religions flog their bodies voluntarily and from the deepest conviction that their God is asking of them, or that it would at least please him well.

In the Islamic month of Muharram about, the rituals of Ashura form the climax of celebrations in honor of the passions of the third Imam Husayn ibn Ali, a grandson of the former prophet Mohammed. In public mourning, believers take part in the sufferings of Husayn and call his fate in parades back in memory. During the execution of the Ashura rituals, there partly happen bodily injuries which cause the believers themselves.

But this form of religiously motivated self-flagellation, which is practiced especially among the Shiites, is not a specialty of Islam.

The mortification is also found in the extreme forms of Christianity, for empathizing the physical and mental suffering of Jesus Christ, more than abound.

So it sometimes the case that people voluntarily are nailed under the guise of a "Compassio" with both hands to the cross.

Here, every person who at least feels to this religion unrelated, arrives to the conclusion that the one who lets himself voluntarily be nailed to the cross in order to empathize the suffering of Jesus Chris, must be totally crazy.

Another manifestation of the religious self-flagellation are the so-called flagellants in medieval Europe. The flagellants are visible on the picture, which precedes this chapter.

The flagellants were a Christian motivated movement of the 13th and 14 Century. They scourged themselves in public places, partly organized in parades, to contribute in this way, to get rid of sins, or simply to kill off their sexual desires. They amused many passersby, while others were simply shocked.

Particularly interesting appears the fact, that some of the flagellants wanted to kill their camal desire by the public sourcing. Today we bring these practices together more with sadomasochism, which does not serve the killing off, but the satisfaction of sexual desires.

Not only today, we realize to what craziness people are sometimes driven by their religious faith, and shake our heads about it rightly.

4.3 "Opium for the People"

"Religion is the sigh of the oppressed creature, the heart of a heartless world, as it is the soul of soulless conditions. It is the opium of the people."

The famous quote from Karl Marx from the "Introduction to the Critique of Hegel's Philosophy of Law" of 1844 goes back to the saying, "Religion is as necessary to man as bread, it is as fatal to him as poison."

Lenin interpreted this statement as the core of the Marxist critique of religion and wrote in 1905 in his book "Socialism and Religion", "Religion is one of the forms of spiritual oppression which everywhere weighs down heavily upon the masses of the people, over burdened by their perpetual work for others, by want and isolation. Impotence of the exploited classes in their struggle against the exploiters just as inevitably gives rise to the belief in a better life after death as impotence of the savage in his battle with nature gives rise to belief in gods, devils, miracles, and the like. Those who toil and live in want all their lives are taught by religion to be submissive and patient while here on earth, and to take comfort in the hope of a heavenly reward. But those who live by the labour of others are taught by religion to practice charity while on earth, thus offering them a very cheap way of justifying their entire existence as exploiters and selling them at a moderate price tickets to well-being in heaven. Religion is opium for the people. Religion is a sort of spiritual booze, in which the slaves of capital drown their human image, their demand for a life more or less worthy of man."

By the way, the comparison between opium and religion, quite apart from the political background, is fully justified, because opium, which was a coming act at that time, makes its user pleasant numbing and euphoric.

Religion has a similar effect. People who are deeply religious are happier people. This is empirically evidenced. The reason for this is seen in the fact, that the religion gives the life of the devout people a meaning.

And this is a very crucial point.

The question of the meaning of one's life turns every right-thinking person in his life, and the religion reflects to have the answer to this oh-so-tantalizing question.

Thus already Einstein said about the meaning of life, "Who sees his own life and that of his fellow men as senseless is not only unfortunate, but also very viable."

That is why everyone has to be aware of the meaning of his own life. Even the ones who are not religious.

Wallace Delois Wattles provides in his books the theory that the purpose of life is to serve our body, our mind and our soul in equal measure. Simple be said, the meaning of life is life itself.

Our bodies and minds we do well know. Only our own souls are difficult to define, and so we ask ourselves what it actually is, the human soul.

And so religious scholars, philosophers, psychologists and psychiatrists make their very own conclusions, and each one has a different definition of "soul" at hand.

Let all these different definitions aside, and let confine ourselves to answer the question of how we can serve our soul.

The religion has always been dealing extensively with the human soul. The German theologian Dietrich Bonhoeffer said, "There is hardly any more complete feeling as to feel that you can be someone for other people." We serve our soul therefore, by giving other people something about security or just a sympathetic ear.

If you are now once more up to decide to stand your loved ones even more aside, you should not proceed as it always religious or political extremists do. Also always want only the best.

4.4 Religious Extremism

For the unbeliever, the common churchy type is usually harmless. However, this changes abruptly as soon as the believer begins to impose his one true religion in a religious extremist delusion upon all others by force.

These extremists form fortunately the exception, but they point in a particularly startling way to the devastating effects of religious delusion.

And so we may rightly fear these religious extremists, whatever their religion is. And we, the freedom-loving ask us again and again, what drives a man to such dangerous religious beliefs.

Religious extremism is not a phenomenon, that only applies to Islam. It is also found in other religions, including Christianity and the Ultra-Orthodox Jews in Israel.

All these religious zealots ignore the strongest an important interpersonal principle:

Everyone, whether he is himself religious or not, should respect the faith of another. And nobody has to interfere unasked in the personal life of another human being. This is especially true in matters of faith. And it applies to everyone - even for adult family members, and for the parents, the children and the own partner.

A failure in observing this principle usually leads to a dispute, because nobody endorse it, if another person wants to dictate him how to lead his life, or what he has to believe. Someone who is not looking for help bucks naturally against such attempts of others to limit his personal freedom.

Finally, we deal with another question, which analyzes the nature of religion in more detail. So we ask ourselves at the end of the chapter "Religion" simply, "Who is God?"

4.5 Who is God?

Completely independent of how we now refer to God, for those who recognize his existence, he is the creator of the universe. He is the one who created us and all life on earth. He is the answer for those who want to know who created the universe, and he gives them hope for an absolutely heavenly life after death. This heavenly life expects the believer after an earthly life full of humility and adoration that is very often act out in magnificently built temples and churches.

Who or what is the creator, who is worshiped regularly in various churches? Nobody quite knows, but the faithful believes, at least, to know it.

And so, anyone who dares draws his very own image of God before his mental eyes.

Albert Einstein, who had always a critical look at religion, painted the following picture of God, "I do not believe in a personal God and I have never denied this but have expressed it clearly. If something is in me which can be called religious then it is the unbounded admiration for the structure of the world so far as our science can reveal it."

Even Sigmund Freud has made his very own image of God. He enters his pioneering psychoanalysis with the belief, that man would see God as a kind of father to whom he could give the responsibility of a self-determined life. This is a process that is controlled by the subconscious mind and is explained by a childlike dependency. He believes that God is nothing else but the satisfaction of an infantile desire for paternal authority and for security.

While Sigmund Freud sees the faith in God as the subconscious satisfaction of a human instinct, others, such as the French writer and philosopher Jean-Paul Sartre, see in God "nothing but a threat to human freedom".

But for those who do not believe in God or the big bang theory, the question remains, who or what created the universe, if it was not created by God, and it has also not created itself with a loud bang.

The famous British physicist and astrophysicist Steph-

Our universe, according to Hawking, has always been there and it will always exist. The universe knows no borders, neither in time nor in space.

Thus, the desperate search for a creator would not be necessary. If the universe never ever had a beginning, then it also needs neither a process of creation nor a creator.

Therefore God exists, as already the poet Bertolt Brecht put it, only in our minds. Therefore this chapter "Religion" concludes with a quote from Bertolt Brecht's book "Tales from Mr. Keuner".

"Someone asked Mr. K. whether there was a God. Mr. K. said: "I advise you to think about whether your be-havior would change depending on the answer to this question. Would it not change, then we can drop the question. Would it change, then I can at least still be ready to help. I'm telling you, you've chosen already. You need a God."

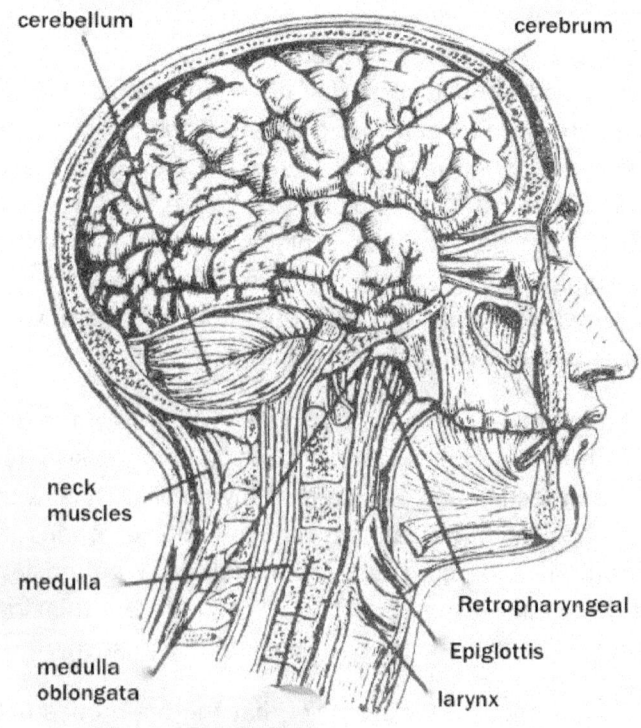

cerebellum

cerebrum

neck
muscles

medulla

medulla
oblongata

Retropharyngeal

Epiglottis

larynx

5. PSYCHOLOGY AND BRAIN RESEARCH

With history, philosophy and religion, we first considered the three sciences, which are quite consistent
in their development. These sciences are extremely
slow to develop.

With psychology and brain research, now the sciences follow that are very dynamic in their present development. The current brain research has reached a climax, and almost every day new, groundbreaking researches are revealed. There are billions of dollars invested in brain research, where even the NASA and the US military are holding vast research projects. Even high-performance athletes benefit in mental trainings of the latest findings in brain research. And now you will begin, no later than now, to take advantage of these valuable insights, too.

The structure of the brain and the functions of the different brain regions are, thanks to progressive research techniques, known in many details. Thus, with the help of MRI scanners thoughts and emotions in the brain can be located and visualized. With this latest techniques we can observe the different thinking processes of the brain and evaluate them exactly.

Today we know, for example, that the brain does not stop to grow, completely independent of the biological age. It is simply wrong that the performance of the brain stagnates or even declines with age. The more the brain is used, the more it develops. It can be trained like a muscle in the body, which is growing by exercising regularly and without assistance again stunting. "You can`t teach an old dog new tricks," this saying is simply not true, because also an "old dog" is able to learn something new.

The brain needs a daily workout at any age and also new challenges. Already now while reading this book, you are training your brain very well and in your brain new neural networks and structures are being created.

At constant challenges, you should lack either. It only depends on how you describe it. Anyone who carries around a bag full of large and small problems can begin to describe his problems no longer as problems but as challenges. His brain and his own person gets an opportunity to grow.

But what is this most complicated mystery of the whole universe, which we call the brain?

The brain is defined as the in the head located part of the central nervous system, and it is mainly composed of nerve tissues and water. This marvel devours an incredible amount of energy and consists of different regions, from which we should know at least the cerebral cortex, the brain stem, the cerebellum, the limbic system and the thalamus.

1. The cerebral cortex, a millimeter-thin wrinkled layer that covers the brain like a cap, is the home to the consciousness and the mind.

2. Our primeval brain, the brain stem governs the vital basic body functions such as breathing and regulating the heart rate.

3. The cerebellum controls all movement routines like walking or grasping with the hand.

4. The limbic system is the home of emotions. It knows us better than we know ourselves.

5. The thalamus is a filter system of the subconscious mind, which decides what is new and important enough to be shared with the awareness.

5.1 The Perception of Reality

The perception of reality is based on the charms of our environment, we perceive with all our senses. We already know that the brain is defined as the in the head located part of our central nervous system. All our senses are directly connected with our brain by countless nerves. Only in the brain, all incoming stimuli are converted in a few milliseconds. This leads, according to our perception, to our very own picture of reality. Thus could be argued, quite possible, that the only place where you have ever been to, is the one in your head.

Allen Snyder, a renowned brain researcher at the Australian Center of the Mind in Sydney concludes from this fact that man can overwrite the reality with his own thoughts. This ability to overwrite and thus to falsify the reality may be, according to Snyder, incredibly powerful.

The image of reality that surrounds us is only in our brains. And that this very own picture of reality, that is produced in our brains, does not necessarily correspond with reality, can be impressively demonstrated by optical illusions and magic tricks, including the following.

The vertical lines that you see in the picture above are obviously to slope, but it turns out on closer look to be a mere illusion. All vertical lines are straight and run absolutely parallel to each other. On the next picture, you can see that the upper part A is clearly less than the lower part B.

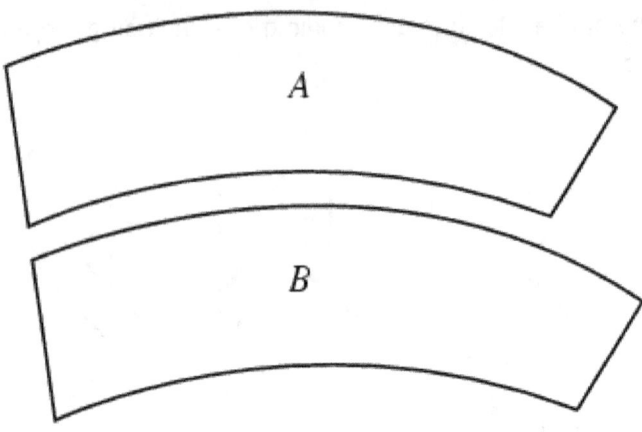

But at this optical illusion, discovered by the American psychologist Joseph Jastrow, the two parts A and B are exactly the same size. They are identical.

After observing the two optical illusions we have to notice, that all we see is not always equivalent to the factual. This applies not only for what we see, but for all our five senses that receive the stimuli in our environment and send them for processing to our brain. This is the first important lesson to reality.

The second important finding considering reality will be, that it is important to distinguish between a reality of the first degree and a second degree reality.

Under the reality of the first degree we understand, for example, the laws of physics and measurement units. No matter what we think about it, these laws and units always remain immutable. A gallon of water is and will always remain a gallon of water, absolutely no matter how you think about that gallon.

Of greater significance for our thinking and our actions is the reality of the second degree. This reality includes our emotions and our personal taste. Furthermore, it includes the all-important question of how we think about the unchanging reality of the first degree, such as in the well known question, whether the water-filled glass is still half full or already half empty.

The irrefutable fact that the reality that surrounds us exists only in our minds is shown by impressive cases of personality disorders, caused by the unconscious processing of a traumatic experience.

5.2 The Processing of a Trauma

How comprehensive the reality that our brain creates really is, in fact, can be demonstrated by cases where a traumatic experience is the reason for the development of a personality disorder. A trauma is defined as an overwhelmingly stressful experience that comes with a sense of death or with a sense of absolute destruction.

Traumatic experiences such brutal rapes involving children can cause immense psychological damage in the form of a so-called dissociation.

With the term of a dissociation the psychologists summarize various disorders of the consciousness and the subconscious mind. A particularly serious case of a dissociation is the identity disorder, which is very often seen in victims of extreme sexual violence in child-hood. Their subconscious mind gives them after the terrible events an entirely new personality. Otherwise these people may not handle well the lessons learned. Their subconscious mind gives them a completely new, or maybe even a second, third or fourth identity.

Your brain tells you, for example, every morning after getting up who are you again. All informations about your true identity can be accessed at any time. You can always rely on it. Always? What happens when your brain, for instance after experiencing a traumatic event or as a result of an epileptic seizure, suddenly puts a spoke on your wheel, and you suddenly get a whole new identity by your subconscious mind?

Please imagine the following incredibly terrifying situation. A group of about ten adults are bullying a small five year old girl with the most brutal torture methods to kill her rabbit, to take out the heart and to eat a piece of it. Another time, she is even forced by her tormentors to do the same with a human baby. Such a scenario, you will think, is probably totally unrealistic, but such statements are reported by victims of satanic rituals. They are often in agreement on this cruel point.

The brains of the children, who were exposed to such cruel situations, constantly form out an identity disorder over time. Is this form of a personality disorder then burst eventually, the victims suffer from the dilemma that this unimaginable horror stories nobody will believe. Instead, these experiences are dismissed as the sheer fantasy of a mental patient.

Thus, an adult woman with a very robust personality suddenly becomes a small, awkward girl who speaks with a childlike voice and loves happy meals from McDonalds. Those affects will change not only their minds by pretending to be someone else, but there are even physical changes such as in the prescription or as in bronchial spasms objectively measurable.

The just described identity disorder makes very clear once again, that reality actually exists only in our brains. Reality does not only include all external influences, but all the internal factors such as the own identity.

This dramatic example brings us in our reflections on the reality, that our brains alone fabricate, a giant step further.

Remember now, against this background, the fantastic children's classic "Alice in Wonderland" by the British author Lewis Carroll, which should be due its numerous adaptations to the most well known. In the picture above, which is taken from the original edition of the book in 1865, we see Alice as a guest at the Mad Tea Party.

The book is about a little girl named Alice who falls asleep bored while her sister is reading from a book. In her dream she curiously follows a talking white rabbit that seems pretty clearly to be late, and therefore it must hurry. In her wild chase Alice meets various oddities and absurdities.

For this reason, many psychologists see Carroll's story as the description of a mind-altering drug trip. Psychologists refer to a particular scene in which Alice has to bite off pieces of the different sides of a fungus. Then she changes according to the bitten side of the fungus her body size.

So it's no surprise that the book title was the name giver for a mental disease. The Alice-in-Wonderland-Syndrome is a combination of coexisting symptoms in which the person perceives himself or his environment changed in a hallucinatory manner. The Alice-in-Wonderland syndrome can be caused not only by the use of mind-altering drugs, but also by a migraine attack or an epileptic seizure.

The syndrome is most often seen in young children. Also Carroll himself suffered as a child under strong migraine. Such migraine attacks, in children`s brains in particular, may lead to various disorders of perception. They often begin to perceive the body as greatly reduced or increased. They begin to see the most fantastic images. Therefore, it is believed that Carroll has also suffered under the Alice-in-Wonderland-Syndrome. What he did put on paper does encourage the idea, that he suffered because of his migraine attacks under hallucinatory perception disorders. Most likely Carroll processed with his book "Alice in Wonderland" his own hallucinations, which seemed so real.

We, however, do neither require a trauma nor a migraine attack, and we also don`t have to eat psychedelic mushrooms in order to overwrite the reality with our thoughts. Ultimately we do not want to create any fantastic dream worlds, but we initially intend to overwrite the reality of the second degree with our thoughts.

However, to find out how we do things when we want to overwrite the reality of the second degree with our thoughts, we must firstly clarify what our thoughts are at all.

5.3 What are Thoughts?

For researchers, the human thoughts are a not decrypted and extremely complex interplay of chemical reactions and electrical voltages that are measurable.

The last point that thoughts can be measured as electrical signals, is particularly interesting, because in this way the mind can be manipulated from the outside. This is also done through the use of electrical signals. Thus, absolutely painless certain regions of the brain can be affected or completely be paralyzed.

In all thinking processes, we must always distinguish between conscious and subconscious thinking processes. We first clarify the question what human consciousness is, before we focus in the following section on the power of the subconscious mind.

The consciousness could be described as the tangible existence of current mental states and processes.

A generally accepted definition of consciousness is very difficult, because the use of the word consciousness is very different. The following European notion of consciousness from the 17th Century shows, that awareness has put people since its discovery by the philosophy before a huge mystery.

For researchers, the awareness is one of the greatest unsolved mysteries of our universe. The philosopher Thomas Metzinger explains the mystery of consciousness as follows, "The problem of consciousness is today, perhaps with the question of the origin of our universe, the extreme limit of human striving for knowledge."

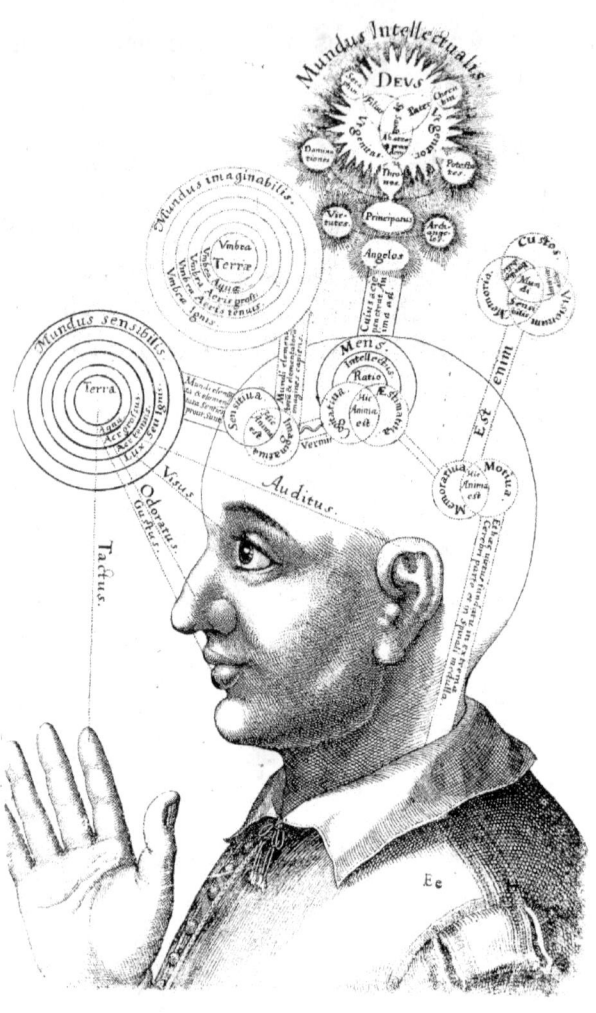

A very well-known and much-discussed phenomenon of our consciousness is the intellect, but in fact it is our subconscious mind, which plays an incredibly powerful role in our daily lives.

5.4 The Power of the Subconscious Mind

About ninety percent of the actions we daily perform are controlled by our subconscious mind. This means that nearly all our actions are more or less automatically transferred into the paths. Our consciousness is usually completely ignored. Our subconscious mind accomplishes true excellence. It controls our motor skills and sorts all the details, that we perceive with our senses, into important and unimportant details. Our subconscious mind always comes out with the best results, which would not occur to us at times, we relied solely on our consciousness and our intellect.

The basis of our subconscious mind is involuntarily our personal life story. So also our personal taste and therefore also our life story is shaped by our subconscious mind.

Our brain constantly tends to do incidental tasks subconsciously. This tendency arises from the fact that "things that go one slight of hand" consume far less energy than conscious thinking processes. Once a new and important questions arises, the awareness is added. The consciousness immediately begins to form new neural networks. This is also the reason why our consciousness needs so much energy. It is constantly creating new neural connections. Even now, in this moment in which you are reading these lines deliberately, your consciousness is creating new connections in your brain. And that, as we already know, in old ages as well as at young ages. This fact clearly shows how adaptable the brain copes with new and unfamiliar tasks.

Because of this fact, more than ninety percent of all our actions are not carried out by our consciousness, but by our subconsciousness. In this way, our subconscious brain dictates us almost all our activities. So many a researchers even claim, that there would be no consciousness. This fact inevitably raises the question of how much influence our consciousness, which is also the home to our free will, ultimately has. Easier would could be wondered,"Who has the control over the whole store?" or just, "Who's the boss?"

The question of who the boss in the store is especially arrises when we are unwilling falling in love and our brain starts to pay out countless happiness hormones. In hardly any other area of life, we depend on the mercy of our subconsciousness as helpless as in love. Though just in the most central areas of our life, our consciousness and our intellect are mostly completely ignored.

But that our subconscious mind as in the case of love, does not only place obstacles in our way, can be proofed upon reading the following simple question:

Wyh sohudl yuo be albe to raed this?

Most people can read this alphabet soup without too much trouble. Your subconscious mind assigns the letters completely automatically and puts them in the right order. Just as your subconscious mind navigates you through the alphabet soup, it navigates you with no further action of your consciousness through your everyday chaos, that surrounds you always and forever.

Our subconscious mind guides us through a world that looks different every day, even if we do not even register, because it is simply not important.

That we do not perceive even the slightest change in our familiar environment, provides an unconscious filter for details, that decides completely without our help, what is attained to our consciousness and thus shared with our attention and what not.

The valuable work done by these subconscious filters shows the following small example of a hayseed in the City. A born hayseed visits for the first time a major city such as New York, Paris or London. He will be overwhelmed by all the new and hectic impressions of the big city. But the more and more he moves through the new city, the more confusing and stressful details are sorted out by his subconscious filters and do not find the attention of the consciousness. So we need this built in subconscious filter system in order to find our way in an increasingly complicated world.

The subconsciousness is therefore responsible for the execution of current tasks, while we can make time travels into the future or into the past in our consciousness. While we revel in memories with our conscious brain, or take a journey into the future, our subconscious mind accepts all well-rehearsed action sequences in the present and pays attention to everything that happens around us. In this way our subconscious gives us the freedom to lose ourselves in our thoughts.

Another important task of our subconscious brain is the scanning of faces. Therefore, the most of our left brain is completely reserved to run this task. Our subconscious mind generalizes new faces so quickly that do not have any significant influence on the results of our subconscious mind. If we include our awareness in the evaluation of a new face, it mostly confirms the previous result of our subconscious mind.

The same applies to all the images that we see. Please take a brief look at the picture below.

What you see is more than just ink on the paper. You do not only see the picture of the New Yorker skyline from the year 1992, but you see everything which you can remember. If you have already once been in New York or if you are living there, an entirely subconscious memory chain is set in motion. If you have been, for example, only once in New York to participate in the marathon, these last images are now aware of your brain. Most of you will probably think of the terror attacks just by seeing the Twin Towers. This memories chains, that are set in motion, could be described as thinking routines.

The already known neuroscientist Allen Snyder calls these routines of thinking mindsets. Snyder is working with high pressure to put these mindsets to expire. He believes that there will be an apparatus in a few years, that lets the world appear in a new light. In this way we will be able to have a world view that is completely free of prejudices. We could see every person we meet, as he really is. Our current prejudiced perception could therefore also be described as a conservative perception.

Please, just take a look at the picture of this man.

Seems pretty freaked out to be.

Now comes the kicker. The man, you see on the picture above, is the very well known brain scientist Allan Snyder, professor at the University of Sydney.

Allan Snyder places a sign against prejudiced thinking, not only with his scientific work, but also with his outer appearance.

We can not trace these subconscious prejudiced thinking routines, that come and go like a passing flock of birds, but if necessary we can try to consciously fight against it.

As we already know, it is possible to overwrite the reality with our thoughts. This applies especially to our subconscious thoughts that initiate virtually all our actions.

This is done by way of the so-called auto-suggestion. The teaching has been developed by the French pharmacist Émile Coué in the 19 Century. Coué discovered that the effect of the medicaments, which he spent on his clients, was heavily influenced by what words he handed them So he came to the conclusion, that a person can increase his well-being, by reciting suggestive formulas, and so he established the doctrine of auto-suggestion.

Auto-suggestive methods work well as a therapy for drug users, including the British bestselling author Allan Carr for the treatment of smokers. With his bestselling book "Easy Way to Stop Smoking" and his equally well-attended seminars, Allan Carr has helped thousands of smokers to successfully get rid of their vice. In his book he repeated like a mantra again and again the benefits of not smoking. The negative effects of smoking, however, are stated at the beginning of the book only in a short passing. This fact clearly shows, that it are positive thoughts that you should include in your own auto-suggestion, and no negative thoughts at all.

The auto-suggestion is a process in which a person trains her own subconscious mind. It is a self-initiated influence of the subconscious mind, which is achieved by mental visualizations, self-hypnosis, meditation or by repetitive affirmations. Probably the most important way to influence one's own subconscious mind is the mental visualization, where you imagine the positive effects of the reaching of your goal as graphic and as accurate as possible. In front your eyes should run a sort of mental film.

The aim of the exercises must be, that these positive beliefs are not only sincerely thought, but that they are also felt. From the idea in your mind a positive feeling has to grow. The more intense the feeling, the better the new idea will be taken over by your subconscious mind.

The mental visualization, which is designed for each person differently, we will take up again in the next part, in which we will have a look at the work of the gifted autistic Temple Grandin, again.

Areas of application of autosuggestion include autogenic training, the mental training and the propagated since the eighties, positive thinking. Autosuggestion is also found in a variety of religious, esoteric or occult rituals. It works by thinking the same thought in the form of the above approaches over a longer period or by repeating it aloud. Often the auto-suggestion is closely related to relaxation techniques. These exercises are repeated until the idea has become an integral part of the subconscious mind. Therefore the initiated the idea can subconsciously lead to appropriate actions. The success of an autosuggestion is more likely the more constant and the more intensive it is applied.

With the help of autosuggestion, you can overwrite the first degree and ultimately also the second degree reality. In this way merge like a beautiful daydream, made of desire and reality.

To find your very own method of autosuggestion is of enormous importance. Because only in this way the subconscious mind can be effectively influenced. And anyone who intends to change his own thinking, and therefore his daily actions and routines must be able to influence his subconscious mind. Finally, it is the subconscious mind, which initiates more than ninety percent of all our actions, we daily perform.

What a gigantic potential our subconscious mind positively hides, can be proofed impressively by the so-called savants.

5.5 The World of a Savant

Yet all too often, people who suffer from a mental disorder are called as "insane". In the Middle Ages, they were persecuted as witches and warlocks, and burned at the stake. Later, they were locked away as asocials together with criminals in asylum centers and workhouses, or they were even abused for the implementation of the kinkiest medical experiments on living people. A humane handling of the "mentally ill" has only prevailed in the wake of the Enlightenment in the late 18th century.

Who looks around in a psychiatric hospital today and talks to the patients, will quickly realize that everyone, such as after an accident, a stroke or a massive blow, may suffer from a mental disorder, and could be accommodated as a result in a psychiatric hospital. We therefore need to meet people who suffer from a mental disorder, with dignity and respect, even though this may not always be easy.

Today we also recognize what amazing abilities sometimes have people who "suffer" from a mental disorder. Of particular interest is the incredible phenomenon of savants. The savants are living in their very own world of facts, figures and systems. More than a half of them are born autistic, and they are brilliant at completely banal facts. For others this ability arises firstly after an accident by which the brain has been damaged. For brain researchers around the world are "those who know" the most sought-after subjects for scientific studies of the vastness of the human brain.

One of the most popular savants by far is the Rainman Kim Peek from Salt Lake City, whose life story was made into a movie in 1988, starring Dustin Hoffman and Tom Cruise in the lead roles. For the embodiment of the autistic Rainman, Dustin Hoffman received the Oscar for best actor.

Although Kim is strongly autistic and therefore considered mentally retarded, he has, like all savants amazingly ingenious, intellectual skills. But even with Kim, it took a long time until he was no longer dismissed as pure insane. Thus, Kim has earned its very descriptive nickname "Kim Computer" honestly. Kim can remember completely unfiltered all the information that he has ever read, seen or heard in his entire life. He was in time like a living universal lexicon or even like a computer, where the delete button is missing. At the age of four, he could recite an entire lexicon after only one reading word by word. In a television quiz show like "Who wants to be a Millionaire" he would have answered the million dollar question with ease and, furthermore, would have told some of the best fitting anecdotes. But despite this extraordinary talent, Kim Peek was not able to independently prepare a fried egg, or even to drive a car. So he lived his life long with his father, Sam Peek.

People like the Rainman Kim are therefore called savants and not geniuses because they also "suffer" from a mental health problem or at least from a cognitive deficit. Sun Kim's brain hemispheres were associated with each other only slightly at birth.

But without a doubt, these savants are geniuses, despite or perhaps precisely because of their mental impairment. Today, the vast majority of researchers believe that many of the great masters, poets and thinkers in history also belong to the circle of savants. The focus has names such as Albert Einstein, Isaac Newton, Sigmund Freud and Alfred Hitchcock up to Wolfgang Amadeus Mozart and Ludwig van Beethoven. Thus we see that even the most famous geniuses "suffered" from a mental disorder. The recognized neuroscientist Michael Fitzgerald of the Trinity College in Dublin is even convinced that only this defect in the brain has made the above figures to geniuses.

Another well-known savant is Steven Wiltshire from Britain. His characteristic nickname is "The Living Camera". Steven also lives like all savants in his very own world. He lives in a world of images. After only a short helicopter ride over a city, that is completely alien to him, he can paint the city to scale and in full detail. He goes back to the exact memory of the last flight over the until then completely unknown city, whether London, Rome and Berlin. While he hears about his ipod disco music of the 70s, he is painting everything as a picture on a large canvas. Steven does not need to exercise. He simply can.

The world of the child prodigy Matt Savange consists, however, not of images but of numbers and music. At the age of seven, he realized the mathematical logic behind the 88 keys on a piano, and so he taught himself to play the piano at a very young age. He began to compose his own jazz pieces. He does not need to practice at all, says Matt, the music is just inside him. The well-known actor and jazz lover Robert De Niro is also a lover of his compositions.

Another interesting figure is the Briton Howard Potter. Howard has a strong interest in prime numbers and football results. He knows all the results with a number of details from countless games. He is not even interested in football and so he does not know the rules of the game. The results of countless games, Howard noted without any effort, but he is not able to explain the penalty rule, because he is only interested in the results. The calculation of mathematical roots have become a daily ritual, which calms his brain. He is combing through the phone book for each prime, but he is unable to make phone calls.

Brain researchers suggest that the savants are able to access their subconscious mind and therefore their entire memories. This circumstance is regarded as the cause of the corresponding island talent. Moreover, the unconscious filter for details lacks in savants. Savants register all details of which our subconscious would filter out the most as unimportant. Do you remember in the previous example from the hayseed in the big city? Gradually his subconscious filter for details is fading out all the exhausting details that brings the city life with out. He can quickly get ever better along the city. Missing our hayseed now this filters for details, as with the Savants, the big-city world always remains exhausting.

In the figure below, for example, autistic people firstly see the twelve single letters and not the whole big letter.

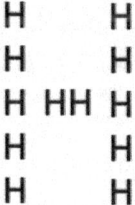

Dr. Darold Treffert of the Wisconsin Medical Society, who has kept himself busy with the phenomenon of savants for years, is a leading expert in the field of the knowing. He and Allen Snyder believe that the skills of an ingenious savant, he has never learned but still has are in each of us. Snyder comes to the startling realization that only certain areas of the brain have to be paralyzed in order to increase the intellectual capacity and also the creativity. He proves this by an experiment in which by means of electrical impulses certain areas in the brain are taken literally off the network. The test subjects have shown after this completely pain-free intervention a significantly increased creativity in the development of strategies. However, according to Snyder, the brain suppresses these skills intentionally.

Snyder also believes that savants see the world as it really is, and explains this among others with the lack of the unconscious filter for details. We, however, would see a world that is constantly trimmed by our subconscious mind.

Particularly noteworthy is the work of the US-American Temple Grandin, also a savants. Her life also became a movie now such as the life of the Rainman Kim Peek. Her work encourages people to think not just about the human thinking, but also about the thinking of animals. The gifted autistic woman who teaches at the University of Colorado, understands bovines and cows immediately. The human emotions are as foreign to her as the recognition of unmistakable facial expressions in faces, such as joy or sadness.

Temple Grandin has encountered during her work, that not every person is capable of imagining a particular situation, for example the opening of your home door and the entering your flat. If you can not think of this everyday situation like a movie, then you are among the small percentage that is not capable of doing.

Some people think fundamentally different and cope with it obviously outstanding. These people most often dispose of other special mental abilities, such as the American physicist and origami artist Robert Lang.

Robert Lang thinks three-dimensionally. He folds from a single sheet of paper, the most amazing figures, such as the following figure shows.

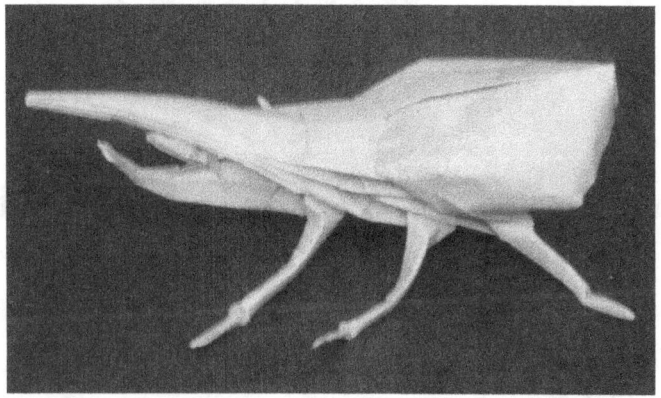

People like Robert Lang think in patterns and models. They are a musicians, mathematicians or physicists, and they can be very often found in places like Silicon Valley.

5.6 The Feelings

Our brain is not only the home to our most intimate thoughts, but also to our feelings. The psychologist Carroll Izard has accurately identified ten different feelings, that occur around the world in every culture. These ten feelings are interest, sorrow, disgust, joy, anger, surprise, shame, fear, contempt, and the feeling of guilt. These feelings can be divided into feelings that are perceived as positive, and feelings that are perceived as negative. The fact that we can make such a division into good and bad feelings, shows that our emotions do always have an evaluative character.

All emotions assess the current situation and are always associated with a greater or lesser change in our own behavior readiness. They motivate us constantly to make certain actions or to refrain from them. Thus, the feeling of anxiety as a warning motivates us either to flee or to attack.

In this case, human emotions then act primarily as initiators of action sequences. On the question of self-motivation, our emotions play therefore a very crucial role.

Apart from the always motivational component, our emotions have numerous other functions:

1. A certain feeling in a part of our body, such as in our bellies or in our limbs, shows us if we feel comfortable in a certain situation or not.

2. Human emotions and their physical affects, such as in the face impression of a person, are an important part of human communication.

3. Our feelings signal to us, whether we are moving in line with the generally accepted social norms and customs.

4. When we are physical or mental stressed, our feelings are signals for overload and stress conditions. In the assessment of our own health and thus also in medicine, our feelings interpret towards the emergence of a disease as well as towards an incipient recovery.

5. Our personal preferences and abilities are influenced by our emotions very much.

6. The feelings have a significant influence on the formation of the reality of the second degree. They make the final decision on their own about view of the world. You could say that we always perceive our world through spectacles of emotions.

7. Moreover, the feelings are some kind of markers for our memories. Each of our memories is marked by a feeling. The more intense the feeling in a sensation was, the better is the memory of the corresponding event.

8. Finally, our emotions have the function to make an assessment of one's own thoughts. This cognitive component of emotions is for our purposes of crucial importance.

Sometimes feelings arise from thoughts, that make an assessment. But our feelings even make an assessment, too. Our emotions always evaluate our thoughts by letting us feel what we should not continue to pursue, or prefer.

Every emotion that is felt to be positive is indicating that you are mentally on the right track. Every emotion that is perceived as negative, however, such as anger or resentment indicates you, that you are mentally on the wrong track.

In this way it is possible to change the ultimate reality of the second degree, positive. An observance of the thoughts, that the emotions have evaluated as a negative, however, inevitably leads to a negative change in the reality of the second degree and, in time, also to a negative change in the reality of the first degree.

Against this background, we shall now consider in detail the emergence of individual feelings. We start with the two strongest emotions of love and hate.

love
Love is seen as the most positive emotion, that we can feel. But brain-technically seen falling in love is nothing but pure stress. When we fall in love fresh, our amygdala, the panic switch our brains gets activated. Our brain begins with a plethora of different happiness hormones like endorphins and several other neurotransmitters. It is this happiness cocktail that ensures that we fall in love, and that we get addicted to the other person over time.

hate and anger

The two related emotions hate and anger are emphasized as deeply negative. Accordingly, these feelings indicate deeply negative thoughts, and negative thoughts are for our purposes absolutely wrong.

But nevertheless, also the negative feelings can be attributed valuable functions.

Who has never felt anger, hate or pain, will never be able to feel happiness or love. It is important to know these feelings and to recognize their valuating character.

An absence of these negative emotions like fear and anger throughout means a also missing of the evaluative component of emotion.

feeling of happiness

With the sensation of happiness, the brain secretes endorphins and the neurotransmitters dopamine and serotonin. The distribution of this euphoric substances is stimulated through various activities, such as through the buzz of sports, through the ingestion of food or even through the performing of the sexual act.

A feeling of happiness also creeps over us whenever we understand something new. Even at the famous "aha" effect our brain begins to distribute auspicious endorphins and neurotransmitters.

The German neuroscientist Gerald Hüther has en-gaged himself for years from a purely brain-technical point of view with the brain phenomenon of learning. Hüther believes that learning is always coupled with a feeling. Enthusiasm and learning are strongly interre-lated. The more we are enthusiastic about something, the easier it is for us to gather the relevant knowl-edge. The grandfather, who falls head over heels in love with a still youthful Swede. But she can only speak Swedish. Now he will learn Swedish with great joy and enthusiasm in no time. For whenever we are enthusiastic about something, we learn almost hands-on new.

But it is fatal when someone firmly believes that he is just not able to do something special, for example math or grammar. This inevitably leads to a negative expectation, and in turn our feelings and our hor-mones come into play.

For example, in the case of the mathematics teacher who tells his student repeatedly on a new one, that he is a dud in math. Sooner or later, this student will be of the firm conviction that he is a single mathematical zero. The return of a class work is done with the usual words, "Well, it was once again nothing." The expecta-tion of the student is confirmed, "I know I'm bad at math." At the same time his brain fatally-wise begins to pour out endorphins for its expectation that nothing will work out in mathematics, has finally been con-firmed. Follows after a long time now but the return of a class with the grade "good", fatally, no endorphins are released.

This example of the bad mathematics student makes clear, how important it generally for someones own development, is which mental image of himself he has. Indeed, it is ultimately that mental picture of yourself, whose form you will sooner or later take. Buddha put this knowledge as follows,

"All that we are is the result of what we have thought. If a man speaks or acts with an evil thought, pain follows him. If a man speaks or acts with a pure thought, happiness follows him, like a shadow that never leaves him. The mind is everything. What we think we become."

feeling of gratitude
The feeling of gratitude is a very positive feeling, that a lot of people seem to have forgotten or never have learned.

Goethe said about gratitude, "If we meet someone who is indebted to us, it directly occurs to us. How often can we meet someone to whom we are indebted, without thinking about it." Do not think about who is indebted to you, but always remember, what you should be grateful for.

Be it your own home, the car in the garage or the cup of coffee and the newspaper in the morning, too many amenities of modern life are simply considered as given. Learn to appreciate the amenities of your daily life, be grateful for these amenities, no matter how small they are.

narcissism

Among the feelings, also false friends cavort like the narcissism. A completely exaggerated narcissism of a man is always expressed in a rigorous quest for power as in the case of dictators. This greed for power over other people, perceived as an outgrowth of self-love, which is fatally emphasized as the-positive, is one of the main weaknesses of mankind.

We find the narcissism not only in dictatorial regimes, but also in the all of us dominating financial world. It is the greed for power over people, which drives a billionaire like Rockefeller to earn more billions.

intuition

Another well-known feeling over its full extent, however, we are not yet fully aware, is the feeling of an intuition.

5.7 The intuition

Intuition is a particularly valuable subconscious function of the human brain. The researchers have just discovered the intuition for themselves. This inner inspiration is a gift of an inestimable value.

The gift of intuition is a foreshadowing of future events, which usually turns out to be correct. It helps us to identify current potentials and opportunities, so that we can use them for us. And the intuition sometimes even leads us to go against existing rules and regulations and notices.

Two spectacular landmark cases in which people have rightly violated time-consuming rules and regulations, are the Apollo Mission and the emergency landing of the plane pilot Chesley Burnett Sullenberger in New York's Hudson River on 15 January 2009. The successful launch of the Apollo 16 space mission in July 1969 would probably have failed without the good intuition of the commander Neil Armstrong. The former fighter pilot changed without obeying any time-consuming rules to manual control. If he had not done so, the onboard computer would have disposed the capsule in a steep crater. Without the intuition of Neil Armstrong the space capsule would probably have never come back. Even the airplane pilot Sullenberger was, like the astronaut Armstrong, an experienced fighter pilot. After a failure of the engines, Sullenberger saved, thanks to his well-trained intuition, all 155 people who were at the time of the accident aboard the plane, their lives.

But despite such encouraging examples, the fact remains that between success and failure is often only a very small degree. In economic and financial matters, it is particularly important, for example, to have a good intuition to sense the future needs of the market. If you are wrong here with your intuition, you may have to pay the price. Especially in business matters, we are depending on a well-trained intuition.

With the creation of our intuition our subconscious mind accomplishes true miracles. It processes all the information stored in our brain and comes in the end to a conclusion that ultimately creeps over us like a feeling and tells us what to do next. By this sense of intuition, you are constantly assailed, and it decides in most cases, what you will do next, as if you are reading this book to its end or not. The intuition has like all our feelings, always an evaluative and motivational character.

Even at the already mentioned automatic facial scan, it is our intuition that signals us if we judge someone to be trustworthy or not. Our intuition has already come to a conclusion, long before we even start to think about this issue. After the conclusion of the intuition, we normally do not use our intellect anymore.

Our brain processes in the development of the intuition all the in the brain stored information, even those information that our consciousness can no longer remember, because it marked the data as simply unimportant, and swapped it into the subconscious mind, more or less. But subconsciously our intuition sends us constantly messages, that affect us in every decision we make.

The intuition of a human being is nothing less than an evaluation of all the experiences and memories, he has accumulated throughout his whole life, utterly regardless of whether he is able to remember consciously or not. Thus the overall experiences and memories of our life determine our intuition and usually also what we will do next.

At this point, we recall once again to the illustration on the cover of this book, the Nautilus, which is increasing her entire life at a constant rate. While it keeps growing, it is constantly creating new wider chambers in perfect proportionality, which are crossed by a lifeline. In this way, the Nautilus returns its previous chambers, but they will never be forgotten. And just as with the steady growth of primeval Nautilus, it is with our thoughts, our experiences, our memories and also with our intuition. We leave all of our thoughts, experiences and memories sooner or later behind, but nothing will ever be forgotten. Everything is stored in our subconscious mind and stays there indelibly our entire lifetime. The more intense our feelings at a certain event were, the faster the event is retrievable by our subconscious mind.

In this way, we reach another valuable lesson.

Individuals train their intuition, by constantly gathering new experiences, thus by breaking out of their familiar environments.

The now following small example illustrates, however, that for the training of our own intuition not only the sole accumulation of new empirical data is sufficient. It also requires constant repetition to save certain processes deep in your subconscious mind. Only by these repetitions, the process will be intuitively quickly accessible. So it is also in the case of bicycle accidents in cities: In cities where many bikes are traveling far fewer accidents with cyclists happen, than in cities with a rather low bicycle traffic. This may seem surprising at first, but the more often the brain of the driver is confronted with cyclists, the faster they are intuitively recognized as a hazard.

The intuition is by far not the only important function of our brain. Other important functions of our brain are the self-control and the motivation. These two related functions can be trained, and therefore they require a closer look.

5.8 Self-Control and Motivation

In the famous "marshmallow study" about self-control and motivation, first held in a research nursery of the Stanford University in San Francisco, four year olds were placed in an extremely difficult position. The children sat down on a chair, and the test administrator presented them two plates on the table. On one plate he put one marshmallow, on the other he put two. Then he faced each child with a difficult decision, "I will leave the room briefly, because I need something done outside. If you wait without calling me until I come back, you will get the plate with the two marshmallows on. If you don`t wait until I get back by myself, you will just get one marshmallow."

Some children devoured their marshmallow immediately after the test administrator had closed the door. Other children began subconsciously with the funniest contortions. In this way, the children dislocated their attention, away from the seductive marshmallows. These children were later in adulthood much more successful and happier in work and family life, than the children who had swallowed their marshmallow immediately.

The brains of the children began completely subconsciously to develop a very unique strategy to resist the temptation. Something in the small children's heads switched to automatic and came to surprisingly good results.

Quite unconsciously the children shifted their perception, just away from the marshmallows, and thus their attention.

This study shows that the "gritting teeth and by" method is the wrong approach. It's a matter of shifting the own attention. This is a very crucial point. We can train ourselves successfully in self-control by shifting our perception and therefore our attention.

About the question of what we put our attention to, we can consciously decide. This sometimes requires some willpower, such as by viewing the image. Take a look at only the white vase, and another time not the vase, but only at the two black faces. A quite difficult task. Looking at this picture, it is almost impossible to shift its attention away from the other object.

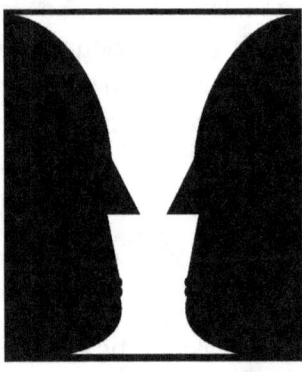

Even magic tricks are always working with the shift of attention.

Self-control and motivation are very closely together. Even if you want to motivate yourself to do something, you have to shift your perception and therefore your attention. But what should be the goal, to which you put your attention to?

Let us remember the human emotions and the best-seller "Easy Way to Stop Smoking" by Allan Carr, which has made thousands of its readers succeed with non-smoking. The positive effects of non-smoking are constantly repeated during the negative effects of smoking are only in a small paragraph ate the beginning mentioned. Formulate all your goals and beliefs positively. So do not be against the use of nuclear power, but be pro the exclusive use of renewable energies. Do not be against child labor, but be pro just good working conditions worldwide. Do not be against the devastating climate change, but be pro a comprehensive climate protection. According to he pure content , both formulations are each the same result.

The crucial difference between the formulations is the following point. In the first formulation you put your attention to the problem, in the second, clearly better formulation, however, you only see the solution. So we have on one hand a clear problem-oriented thinking, and on the other hand a clear solution-oriented thinking. If you do not only want to perform a limbo about your problems, you need to describe your problems no longer as problems, but as possibilities for your own improvement . There is always a solution.

Therefore, avoid most entirely the phrase "I am opposed to ...", but instead use the phrase "I'm in favor, that ..". Finally, your choice of words is a very crucial sign of how you even think about things.

This is a very good way to train your solution-oriented thinking. Also the number of your problems will shrink by these simple reformulation very much, and you will get faster to a solution-oriented thinking on the necessary solutions. You can ultimately act effectively.

5.9 From Thinking to Acting

If you begin, after reading this book, to guide your thoughts in a completely new way, you have already taken the biggest step. This will be a really hard training. But if your imaginary thoughts do not also lead to any action, you will just remain a builder of castles in the air, and in your life, despite the new thoughts, nothing will turn for the better. "A thought which does not lead to action is not much," said George Bernardo, "and an act which does not proceed from a thought is nothing at all." So you must also begin to act in accordance with your new thoughts. Otherwise, your desires are nothing but just bubbles, which burst in the air.

"The one waits that the time changes and other acts," once said the Italian poet and philosopher Dante Alighieri. But far worse and worse for the society are not the for the course of time waiting, but it are those who act completely reckless.

Another unpleasant phenomenon are the self-appointed teachers, no one has called in to help. These are people who like to interfere unasked in the life of another human being, because they suppose to know what is best for him. This human kind is generally not very popular with their fellow men. The remarkable thing is, that these people would also view it as outrageous, if someone interferes unasked in their own private lives. Even the great Chinese philosopher Confucius used to say,

"Demand much of yourself and expect little of others. Ye shall be spared much trouble."

Therefore, it is the best not even to criticize other people's ways of thinking, but to take it with humor, and to be just a good role model for them. The Irish writer and poet Oliver Goldsmith said in this regard, "You can preach a better sermon with your life than with your lips."

The German neuroscientist Gerald Hüther thinks that we have a problem of implementation. I think that the problem is already in the lack of knowledge of the valuable findings of brain research. This knowledge about the capabilities of the brain is in our schools (in Europe), unfortunately, not part of a curriculum. It lacks a targeted distribution of this knowledge. Only the one who has this knowledge can ultimately realize it. The American psychologist Carol Dwek was able to demonstrate with numerous studies that after a transfer of scientific knowledge about the brain and the intelligence, the process of learning in schools leads to higher learning outcomes in students. The new-found conviction of a student that he can be better in any subject, is often enough to improve his grades.

But the knowledge of the latest brain research alone is not enough. These findings also need to be implemented. So if you ultimately want to act effectively, you must have a big goal that you have set for yourself and that you are working towards. This means that you must firstly be able to identify your own personal goal as clear as possible. Without a clear goal, which indicates the direction of your life, you will not even see the opportunities that are abundant. So already the Roman philosopher, scientist and statesman Seneca knew,

"When a man does not know what harbor he is making for, no wind is the right wind."

The achievement of this self-imposed goal is to ensure that we meet or even gives happiness.

Various psychological studies have shown, that different factors play a crucial role in achieving the self-set goal:

1. Concrete Formulation of the Goal

Many people fail already at identifying their own goals in concrete terms. It is not too difficult to name the own vast concrete goal. Exercise, weight loss and learning are certainly worthy goals, but they are formulated much too vague. The consequence of these vague formulations is, that the strategies and plans that emerge from it, are just as fuzzy and vague. "If I want to reach my goal, I only have to give my best," the psychologist Heidi Grant Halvorson is convinced that these vague formulations are demonstrably "not effective", but the best way to mediocrity.

Name your target so as accurately as possible and as precisely as possible. What physical activity is exercised when and where, how many pounds are taken off when, and what is learned by what and by when?

In this way you can imagine a huge, detailed and motivating picture of your goal that will attract you almost magically. In this manner, the precisely shaped picture of the achievement of your goal tells you what your personal vision is.

2. The Time Factor

To designate time and place as accurately as possible is the most effective method, which contributes to the success of a plan. This exact plan stimulates the brain to create the right connections, which help that the plan is adhered to and implemented. You will, in particular for short-term goals, not ask why you need to do something, but just what you have to do when and where. This brings a very huge advantage. You reduce the complexity of your overall goal. You begin to look exactly how to get from point A to point B. One point is always followed by another point.

3. Self-Knowledge

Another important factor is the factor of self-knowledge. Self-knowledge requires a minimum level of self-reflection.

To achieve your goal, you need some willpower. Researchers discovered that there is a psychological barrier of willpower. It is not a bottomless reservoir of power. Our own willpower has limits. Be aware of, that there are borders of your own willpower.

The good news is that the strength of will can, as described in the part about self-control and motivation, be trained. When you exercise your willpower in this way, you will soon be able to maintain a high degree of willpower over time.

4. Realism

Always stay realistic. This applies both, for the objective and for the achievement of the objective.

In a realistic assessment of our projects, in turn, our feelings help us, both positive and negative feelings. If you think of what the consequences of a failure are, you can see what the possible obstacles on your way to your destination are. Do expect setbacks. They are inevitable. The more ambitious your goal, the more you must also expect setbacks.

5. The Need for Autonomy

According to the so-called self-determination theory of the psychologists Edward Deci and Richard Ryan, the intended goal should serve the satisfying of three basic human needs. In this way, the persuasion of the goal leads to a lasting bliss. These three basic human needs are autonomy, competence and relatedness.

When it comes to your personal life or your goal, you naturally want to decide as much as you possible by yourself. This quest for the greatest possible autonomy is a basic human need, which you should consider when you set your own goal.

You want to live and not to be lived. That is how Walter Kohl, son of the former German Chancellor Helmut Kohl formulated it.

Psychologists can prove in numerous studies that already the impression that the goal was self-selected, is sufficient to increase the creativity and the endurance significantly. Be autonomous in your goals. Being autonomous means in its word origin "to give yourself laws".

The law that you impose on yourself to be totally autonomous, is the goal towards you are working.

6. The Need for Competence

The second basic need that guarantees happiness in life, is the competence factor. The need for competence is to experience one's own efficacy. It is the desire to influence his environment with his skills in some form. It is the deep-rooted in the human desire to shape his environment with his very special abilities.

And how do you want to shape your environment with a lot of enthusiasm?

7. The Need for Relatedness

The third and final factor is the basic need for love or relatedness. It is the desire to love and to be loved. It is the basic human need for intimate and intense relationships with other people. This desire for relatedness is the reason why we go to clubs, and why we frolic at parties and on social networks like facebook. Remember to acquire this third basic need for relatedness with your personal goals to reach a lasting happiness after achieving the self chosen goal.

8. The Development of the Full Potential

The setting of the personal goal is not about impressing others, for example by obtaining some doctor`s degree. It is important that you reach your full potential, also in achieving a doctor`s degree. The developing of your full potential is the really important point.

The already known psychologist Carol Dwek of the Stanford University has found, that there are two fundamentally different beliefs by which people evaluate their own skills and talents.

Do you personally think, that's just the way you are or do you believe, that everything can be changed, the language, the fitness, the memory and much more?

The first group, Carol Dwek calls the "property theorists". The second group is called the "growth theorists". At least after reading this book, you should also belong to the second group, the group of growth theorists. Growth theorists see their ambitious goals rather than an impending overload, but more as an opportunity for their personal growth. By setbacks that are at a challenging target almost inevitable, these people can not be discouraged.

The claim to yourself as a growth theorist should therefore be, "Difficult, but doable". That is at least how the psychologists Edwin Locke and Gary Latham formulated it after an extensive study. According to Locke and Latham through an ambitious and clearly defined goal, the effect of a so-called high-performance spiral is started up. Just make sure that you still remain realistic in your challenging goals.

There needs to be a hard workout to unlearn old habits, and to replace them with new, well-designed and targeted habits. The same is true especially for the old habitual thinking, of course.

But already working towards your goal will make you quickly more satisfied, happier and much more confident. In this way, an ambitious target is followed by an even more challenging.

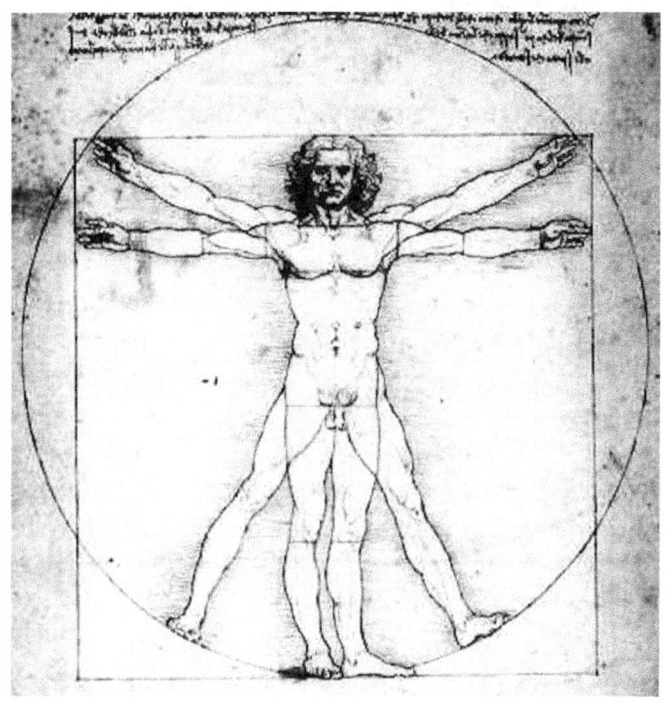

6. MEDICINE

In the medical field we are interested in the two main processes of our body that are associated with our mind. This is on the one hand the process of getting ill and on the other hand the subsequent process of recovery.

So we firstly look at psychically related physical ailments and subsequent at the so-called placebo effect.

6.1 Psychologically Related Physical Sufferings

In the discussion of mentally caused physical suffering, we have to notice that mental disorders, such as depression or stress disorders have increased rapidly for years.

If in the lives of those affected sooner or later arrises a serious crisis, they completely collapse. It is therefore particularly important to train his own mind that it is strengthen to the everyday stress as much as possible. Too many people are limited to make their bodies more resilient by making sport and by eating right against possible diseases, and neglect altogether the right training for their mind. Taking care of your mind is at least as important as taking care of your body, if not even more important.

Body and mind form an indivisible whole, and it is mostly the mind that shapes the body. It is the mind that decides which food is supplied to the body and which sport takes place.

The unity of mind and body can already be illustrated by numerous phrases. Thus in a state of high anxiety, "I heart beats up to his neck," or, "I have a lump in my throat." For particularly large lovesickness "breaks your heart", and the one who is ashamed or angry, turns red. In particular, our voice varies widely according to our own feelings. Our voice reveals our emotional state as well as our entire language. The inseparable unity of body and mind is also manifested in some disease states. When they arise, the mind plays a very crucial role. But not every disease is, as about Scientologists claim, a false thinking owed. There are many diseases whose releases are not to be found in the mind. For other physical illnesses such as the peptic ulcer disease, however, a mental health problem is considered to be pathogenic.

The peptic ulcer disease is a tissue defect in the duodenum, resulting in abdominal pain, fasting pain and severe nausea. Mostly it is chronic and recurring. The peptic ulcer disease is closely associated with psychosocial problems, as they occur in a professional or private overload.

Sufferers seem therefore not to be able to deal with poor professional and personal stress very well, because on one side they feel a strong urge for independence, but on the other side they also lead to dependence. Thus the person gets into an ongoing internal conflict, that wears him down. This inner conflict is regarded as the cause for the emergence of peptic ulcer diseases.

Another physical suffering, that is largely responsible for the development and course of psychological symptoms, is known as the crohn's disease, a chronic inflammation that comes from the small intestine. Regularly it makes itself felt with diarrhea, fever, abdominal pain, decreased appetite and thus weight loss. It only rarely heals again. Triggers are psychosomatic factors, such as significant separation anxiety.

Thus, the treatment of the crohn's disease is mostly supported by psycho-therapeutic measures.

From the plagued digestive to the airways. The bronchial asthma is a spastic contraction of the bronchial muscles, the accumulated abundant mucus. In addition to plant-related causes, disturbances of an early mother-child relationship seems to be the cause for the disease.

Through the skin, diseases of the mind are visible. Sun psychological factors also contribute in the development of atopic dermatitis, a recurring itchy skin condition. The persons concerned have described a lack of emotional support in childhood, but also an external over-protection. Many act in their whole personality cautious, sensitive and in fear of contact. In addition to the dermatological treatment of the affected skin, patients are usually accompanied with psychotherapy.

"An untrained brain is more harmful to health than an untrained body," said the aforementioned Irish writer and poet George Bernard Shaw. We keep this quote in mind as we now turn to the well known placebo effect.

6.2 The Placebo Effect

Already historical time patients were treated by pure discuss. The Greek philosopher Plato was the belief that words have quite the power to heal people. Plato thus legitimized the lie of medical placebos. It is perfectly acceptable that seriously ill patients are given against better judgment, the feeling that there are still chances of a cure, or that his illness was not nearly as bad as he might think.

But Plato's belief contradicts the popular notion of a good medical treatment. Hippocrates, an outstanding physician of his time, had the opinion that the success of an administered drug can not be pinned down to the personal efforts of the treating physician, but only to the strict adherence to the rules of medical science.

Today clarifies the doctor his patients extensively on the established disease and the further treatment, "We have discovered an extremely malignant cancer that is already in the final stage. To this day there is still no treatment that is able to stop the deadly course of the disease. In all likelihood, you will have to live two, maybe even three years." In legal terms, he did well, but from a purely medical and course of brain-technical point of view, this statement, according to Plato, is highly fatal.

But what is this salutary placebo effect? The placebo effect, which was also blamed for causing numerous religious miracle is based on the administration of a placebo. A placebo in the narrow sense is a sham drug, which itself contains no drug and therefore can not exhibit any pharmacological activity. In a broader sense with placebo, other sham interventions, such as a sham operation, are meant.

The placebo effect is an improvement of the subjective condition of measurable bodily functions, which are attributed to the previous sham treatment.

Particularly interesting is the fact that the placebo effect does not only occur in sham interventions, but also in proper medical procedures. In this way, the placebo effect has a greater or lesser influence over each treatment success, based on a medical intervention. Today rarely pure or complementary placebo therapies are used in clinical practice. Especially great is the success of a placebo therapy in the relief of pain.

In the past, the researchers could only partially explain, how the placebo effect exerts its beneficial effects. That has changed with the turn of the millennium fundamentally. Brain researchers were able to use the latest scanner technology with people who were open to placebos. They found an enormous release of the neurotransmitter dopamine. The increased level of dopamine is the reason, why the belief in healing sometimes causes more than just taking a drug. The placebo effect has become an integral component in basic medical courses at universities across the country. Also shamans and healers know about the power of the redemptive placebo effect. This leads very often a mere sham acupuncture treatment to the desired success.

The counterpart of the placebo effect is called the nocebo effect. The nocebo effect is a negative reaction of the patient, which is not due to the effects or side effects of the treatment, but solely on its psychosocial context.

If we transfer the knowledge, gained through our feelings from the previous chapter "Psychology and Brain Research" on the placebo effect, this means that in the case of an illness, you only should keep the positive consequences of entering recovery in mind.

The basic principle is: The body and the mind form an indivisible whole. The mind forms the body and the body in turn forms the brain.

7. NATURE SCIENCES

The previous studies have promoted the elaboration of the principles of mindleading already in large and decisive steps.

Finally, now the nature sciences will make their important contribution to the elaboration of the fundamentals.

Of particular interest in the field of natural sciences are physics, represented by Albert Einstein, and biology and genetics.

7.1 Einstein about Energy

$$E = mc^2$$

Albert Einstein's most famous formula of the world, translated literally reads as follows: The rest energy of a body is equal to its mass multiplied by the speed of light squared.

The square of the speed of light is a fixed size. The speed of light is always the same. The energy and mass, however, are variable sizes. Mathematically speaking, these two quantities are equivalent. That means for the physical reality, which is the reality of the first degree, that the mass is nothing but concentrated energy in their original state.

Anything that has a mass is energy in the idle state. Everything that surrounds us is mass, not transformed energy in a concentrated form. It always takes this same energy in many forms: a stone, a tree, an entire rainforest, a faithful dog or a cat.

The highest form that this energy can take, is the form of a human with his unique brain. Thus the always same original substance from which the monists among philosophers speak, gets a new name: energy.

Everything is energy in various forms.

Also in the process of thinking is mass, mainly sugar-energy is converted into energy, which is then released as a thinking process. This energy, which releases the brain, can be measured.

Against this background, the theory of relativity by Albert Einstein could be added another theory:

Energy = Thought

This always the same energy that can think, must obey certain fixed predetermined rules. This energy must obey the laws of nature, for otherwise our universe as we know it would not exist.

If this energy must obey fixed predetermined rules, then our thoughts, also energy, must also be the subject to fixed laws of nature.

The power of our thoughts can be measured in frequencies. Every thought sends out a different frequency. In this way, it must be able to act on energy. Energy has an influence to each other. The crucial question is therefore, to which inherent nature laws the energy is affected.

Since the new thought movement it is spoken more by a law of attraction or the law of resonance, after the same attracts the same. This assumption is based on the relationship between the thoughts and feelings of a person to the personal circumstances.

The law of resonance is thus based on an analogy between mental processes and external influences. If this law is indeed true, this irrefutable law of nature opens each of its users almost unbelievable possibilities. If this law actually exists, is not proven to this day. It just remains a theory.

The good news is now: If you follow only the principles worked out in this book, then the law of resonance, if it should really exist, will also work for you.

7.2 Biology and Genetics

In the field of biology, the science of life, we are interested in particular the principle of growth, that is inherent in nature. At this incessant growth as a part of nature, the at a constant rate growing nautilus reminds us symbolically .

The principle of growth also illustrates a seed, which is set to germinate in the soil. The seed, that does not lives, but that carries life in itself becomes active and begins to grow. According to the law of life this seed produces many other seeds. In this way, life with life, it multiplies itself to keep growing, and it must constantly grow if it wants to exist at all. So it is aptly called in an old Jewish saying:

"If you're not growing, you're getting smaller."

The principle of perpetual growth, which is carried in

all life, can be easily transferred to our own thoughts. Even with our thoughts, we almost helpless subject to the natural principle of perpetual growth.

On every thought we think follows another thought, and each learned is followed by the learning of subsequent findings. Expand our consciousness as well as our subconscious is constantly and incessantly.

If you have a good idea, then write down this idea, and you will see that you will soon have a whole sheet full of ideas. One good idea follows the other.

That this biological principle of growth is inherent to the human mind, the many groundbreaking scientific achievements, not at least the deciphering of the genetic code, demonstrate.

The Welsh mountain sheep Dolly, born on the 5th June 1996, proves that it is possible to clone human beings.

It is a particularly clear example for the incredible abilities of the human mind. It also raises the question of where the boundary of the growth of the human mind is, if it even exists.

Man is taking walks on the moon, is surfing the world wide web with high-tech mobile phones and is able to clone animals. So it seems to be that for the human mind obviously no limits to growth exist. The human mind keeps growing, and it does so with such a rapid rate that it can make one dizzy.

The human mind has no limits at all.

And also in your mind, the principle of perpetual growth is firmly established, and the only person that can limit this growth, is you. Only you.

Your personal goals determine the boundaries of your own growth. If your personal goals are sticked too low and then reachable with ease, you will never be able to discover that there are also no limits to your growth, except perhaps those that you have previously pulled yourself.

You can choose yourself the direction in which your mind grows. This important decision, you should not leave to other people. Only you can expand the boundaries and thus the possibilities of your own growth. This important decision can and should relieve you of anyone.

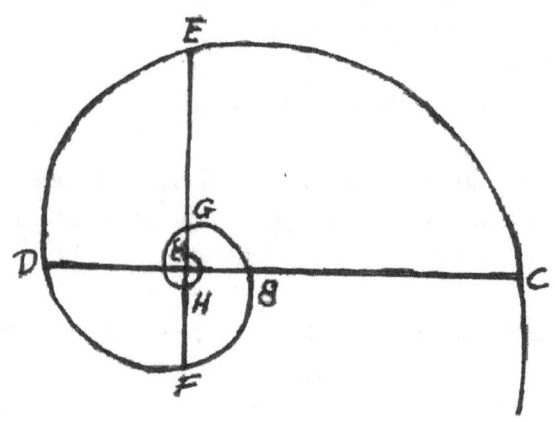

8. THE PRINCIPLES OF MINDLEADING

The Science of Mindleading shows if and how a person is able to lead his own thoughts on the desire to act effectively in any situation and to become a successful and happy people. For this purpose, the Science of Mindleading evaluates the knowledges of all the well-established sciences and links them together.

The basic result of this evaluation are the following ten Principles of Mindleading.

§ 1 Conduct of Life

You can only change yourself and not your fellow citizens. Meddling in the life of another human being, be he ever so familiar, should be completely avoided. This is done by adopting the role of a model and not the role of a great teacher, who meddles always unasked. Expect a lot from yourself and only little from others.

§ 2 The Meaning of Life

The meaning of life is very plain and simple the life itself. Just live by serving your body, your mind and your soul in equal measure.

§ 3 The Reality

Each brain manufactures its very own picture of reality. We have to distinguish between a first degree and a second degree reality. The reality of the first degree, such as physical units are mentally not directly influential. The all-important reality of the second degree, as our feelings and beliefs can, however, easily be overwritten by our thoughts. This requires that deadlocked subconscious thinking routines can be overcome and replaced by new ones. If this is successful, over time, the reality of the first degree will get closer to the reality of the second degree.

§ 4 The Subconscious Mind

Our thinking routines and almost all our daily actions are initiated by the subconscious mind. Therefore you can only change your own thinking substantially by affecting your subconscious mind. This is done mainly with the help of auto-suggestive visualizations. In such mental visualizations you imagine the positive effects of your reached goal as graphic and as accurately as possible. Before your eyes should run a sort of mental film.

§ 5 The Language

Pay attention to your verbal formulations. They provide a lot of information about your thinking patterns. You should therefore always use positive formulations and no negative. These positive formulations promote your solution-oriented thinking enormously.

§ 6 The Emotions

The feelings are always able to conduct a review of one's thoughts. Emotions that we feel as a positive show us, that we are mentally right. Negative emotions show us, however, this idea should not considered further.

§ 7 Goals in Life

We must train ourselves constantly in self-control and motivation, so also with our personal priorities. By achieving these goals, the three basic human needs of autonomy, competence and relatedness should be satisfied. After a self-reflection, your own goal should correspond to your own capabilities and allow you to reach your full potential. When you have found your goal, you should name it as clearly and precisely as possible.

§ 8 The Image of Yourself

The life goals you have set for yourself, reflect the mental image of yourself. In this way, it will be exactly that mental picture of yourself, whose form you will actually take over time.

§ 9 The Intuition

Also you have in certain matters in which you are particularly skilled, a good intuition. One's intuition is trained by constantly creating new experiences and excavating from the usual and familiar environment.

§ 10 The Principle of Growth

Also, your thoughts subject almost helplessly to the natural principle of continuous growth. The brain does not cease to grow, and therefore it is up to the brain of each user to decide for itself, in which direction it wants to grow.

With the fundamental principles of the Science of Mindleading, you are now familiar. In the second volume of the Science of Mindleading, these fundamental findings will be reiterated and reinforced.

The Science of Mindleading Volume II with the subtitle "The Intelligence" will deal with the issues of education and learning. Today, standardized intelligence tests decide on the educational, the academic and the professional future of millions of people in many countries. They decide on the inclusion in special education programs for gifted children, on the award of grants to higher education institutions, on the setting in a company or on the targeted use of recruits in the military. The intelligence characterizes a people more than any other personality trait. Get together with the Science of Mindleading to the bottom of the cognitive performance. Is it possible to improve your intelligence, perhaps even at an advanced age?

This second book will tell you.

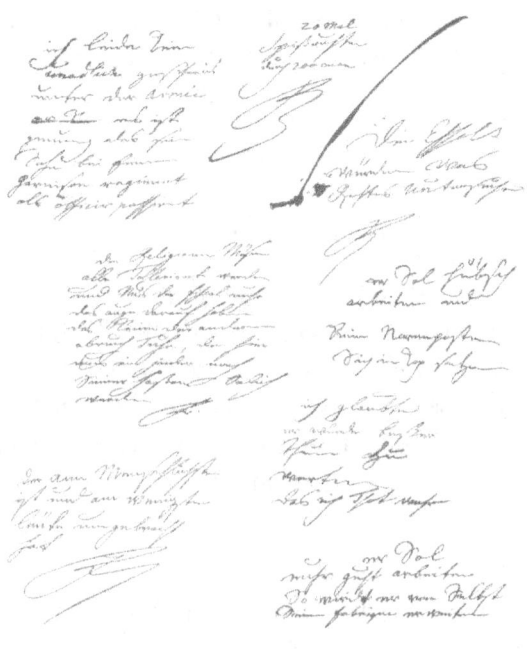

9. QUOTES

The final small collection of quotes from famous and recognized personalities in history shows very clearly once again, that the basic ideas of a Science of Mindleading are far from new.

George Bernado

"A thought which does not lead to action is not much and an act which does not proceed from a thought is nothing at all."

Buddha

"All that we are is the result of what we have thought. If a man speaks or acts with an evil thought, pain follows him. If a man speaks or acts with a pure thought, happiness follows him, like a shadow that never leaves him. The mind is everything. What we think we become."

William Ellery Channing

"All that man is external, is finally the expression and completion of his inward thought. To work effectively, he needs to think clearly. To act nobly, he must think nobly."

Winston Churchill

"You create your own universe as you go along."

Confucius

"Demand much of yourself and expect little of others.
Ye shall be spared much trouble."

Francois-Urbain Domergue

"Some people study all their lives, and at their death
they have learned everything except to think."

Marie von Ebner-Eschenbach

"If there is a faith that can move mountains, it is the
belief in one's own strength."

Albert Einstein

"I do not believe in a personal God and I have never
denied this but have expressed it clearly. If something
is in me which can be called religious then it is the unbounded admiration for the structure of the world so
far as our science can reveal it."

Ralph Waldo Emerson

"The key to every man is his thought. Sturdy and defying though he look, he has a helm which he obeys, which is the idea after which all his facts are classified. He can only be reformed by showing him a new idea which commands his own."

Johann Wolfgang von Goethe

"All truly wise thoughts have been thought already thousands of times; but to make them truly ours, we must think them over again honestly, until they take root in our personal experience."

Oliver Goldsmith

"You can preach a better sermon with your life than with your lips."

Oliver Wendell Holmes

"A mind that is stretched by a new experience can never go back to its old dimensions."

Arthur Schopenhauer

"We may divide thinkers into those who think for themselves and those who think through others. The latter are the rule and the former the exception. The first are original thinkers in a double sense, and egotists in the noblest meaning of the word."

Seneca

"When a man does not know what harbor he is making for, no wind is the right wind."

George Bernard Shaw

"An untrained brain is more harmful than an untrained body."

J.W. Teal

"It is the habitual thought that frames itself into our life. It affects us even more than our intimate social relations do. Our confidential friends have not so much to do in shaping our lives as the thoughts have which we harbor."

ABOUT ME, FELIX BROCKER

I was born in Viersen, a small town on the lower German Rhine, and I began after obtaining the baccalaureate to study law at the Ruhr-University Bochum and at the Johannes Gutenberg University in Mainz, with a focus on culture and media law. During my training, I did several internships, so in the press office of the Parliament of Rhineland-Palatinate, the Ministry of the Interior and Sports of Rhineland-Palatinate, the state police, at police headquarters in Mainz and at a law firm.

During my studies I worked extensively with the human mind and its implications. This led me inevitably to the fundamental questions of life. Who or what created the universe and what is the meaning of life?

I translated this book completely by myself. I am not a native speaker, but I love the English language. Therefore I ask you, if you have spotted any mistakes. If so, please let me know and send me an email to

info@science-of-mindleading.com

I wish you, dear reader, a fascinating and insightful read,

Felix Brocker

www.ingramcontent.com/pod-product-compliance
Lightning Source LLC
Chambersburg PA
CBHW072329290526
45794CB00002B/793